Essential Software Design
JavaScript Developers

• 1 Introduction 1

• 2.1 The Role of Patterns in Software Development...............2

• 2.2 Patterns - Common Misconceptions 3

• 2.3 Patterns - Patterns vs. Frameworks 3

• 2.4 Patterns - How to Think About Patterns 3

• 3 Singleton – The One and Only...4

• 3.1 Singleton - What the Singleton Solves...........................4

• 3.2 Singleton - When and Why to Use a Singleton...............5

• 3.3 Singleton - How to Implement a Singleton (in JS) 5

• 13.4 State - Visual Diagram 7

• 12.4 Command - Visual Diagram 7

• 11.4 Strategy - Visual Diagram...7

• 10.4 Observer - Visual Diagram 7

• 9.4 Proxy - Visual Diagram 7

• 8.4 Decorator - Visual Diagram 7

• 7.4 Facade - Visual Diagram..7

• 6.4 Adapter - Visual Diagram 7

• 5.4 Prototype - Visual Diagram 7

• 4.4 Factory - Visual Diagram...7

• 3.4 Singleton - Visual Diagram..7

• 3.5 Singleton - Analogy Recap 7

• 3.6 Singleton - Pitfalls and Misuse 8

• 4 Factory – Manufacturing Objects on Demand 8

• 13.1 State - What Problem Does It Solve?...........................9

• 12.1 Command - What Problem Does It Solve? 9

• 11.1 Strategy - What Problem Does It Solve? 9

• 10.1 Observer - What Problem Does It Solve? 9

• 9.1 Proxy - What Problem Does It Solve? 9

• 8.1 Decorator - What Problem Does It Solve?..................................9

• 7.1 Facade - What Problem Does It Solve? 9

• 7.2 Facade - When and why use a Facade...................................9

• 6.1 Adapter - What Problem Does It Solve?..................................9

• 5.1 Prototype - What Problem Does It Solve? 9

• 4.1 Factory - What Problem Does It Solve? 9

• 4.2 Factory - When and Why to Use a Factory..................................9

• 4.3 Factory - How it Works..................................10

• 13.5 State - Analogy..................................12

• 12.5 Command - Analogy 12

• 11.5 Strategy - Analogy 12

• 10.5 Observer - Analogy 12

• 9.5 Proxy - Analogy 12

• 8.5 Decorator - Analogy..................................12

• 7.5 Facade - Analogy 12

• 6.5 Adapter - Analogy 12

• 5.5 Prototype - Analogy 12

• 4.5 Factory - Analogy 12

• 4.6 Factory - Pitfalls and Considerations 12

• 5 Prototype – Cloning the Blueprint 13

• 5.2 Prototype - When and Why to Use Prototype..................................13

• 5.3 Prototype - How to Implement Prototype in JS 14

• 13.6 State - Pitfalls 16

• 12.6 Command - Pitfalls 16

• 11.6 Strategy - Pitfalls 16

• 10.6 Observer - Pitfalls 16

• 9.6 Proxy - Pitfalls..................................16

• 8.6 Decorator - Pitfalls 16

• 7.6 Facade - Pitfalls..16

• 6.6 Adapter - Pitfalls...16

• 5.6 Prototype - Pitfalls..16

• 6 Adapter – Making Incompatible Interfaces Work Together.......18

• 6.2 Adapter - When and Why to Use Adapter 18

• 6.3 Adapter - How to Implement Adapter in JS............................19

• 7 Facade – A Simplified Interface to a Complex System 22

• 7.3 Facade - How to Implement Facade in JS...............................24

• 8 Decorator – Adding Functionality Without Subclassing 28

• 8.2 Decorator - When and Why to Use Decorator.........................29

• 8.3 Decorator - How to Implement Decorator in JS 29

• 9 Proxy – The Object Stand-in (The Middleman)..........................35

• 9.2 Proxy - When and Why to Use Proxy 36

• 9.3 Proxy - How to Implement..37

• 10 Observer – Keeping Objects in the Loop 42

• 10.2 Observer - When and Why to Use Observer..........................43

• 10.3 Observer - How to Implement Observer in JS 43

• 11 Strategy – Different Ways to Do the Same Thing 47

• 11.2 Strategy - When and Why to Use Strategy 49

• 11.3 Strategy - How to Implement Strategy in JS.........................49

• 12 Command – Encapsulating Actions as Objects 54

• 12.2 Command - When and Why to Use Command........................55

• 12.3 Command - How to Implement Command in JS 56

• 13 State – An Object with Many Faces..61

• 13.2 State - When and Why to Use State 62

• 13.3 State - How to Implement State in JS 63

• 14 Conclusion...70

Introduction

Software design patterns are like time-tested playbooks for common coding problems. They aren't concrete code, but rather **reusable solutions** to recurring design issues that developers face. Think of them as blueprints: they describe how to structure your code to solve certain problems in a clean, maintainable way. These patterns became famous after the "Gang of Four" (GoF) published *Design Patterns: Elements of Reusable Object-Oriented Software* in 1994, cataloging 23 classic solutions. Ever since, developers have used this shared vocabulary of patterns to design new systems and quickly understand existing ones.

Here's the thing: even though JavaScript isn't a purely class-based language like Java or C++, its flexible nature still lets us implement these patterns (often with functions or ES6 classes). In fact, you've probably *used* some of them without realizing it. The goal of this book is to shine a light on these essential patterns – from the simplest to the more advanced – and show how they apply to JavaScript development, making you a better JavaScript coder. We'll explore **creational** patterns (ways to create objects), **structural** patterns (ways to organize object relationships), and **behavioral** patterns (ways to manage communication between objects), in a language everyone can understand, from junior to senior.

Each chapter will dive into one design pattern. We'll cover what the pattern is and the problem it solves, when and why you would reach for it, and how it works under the hood. Expect JavaScript code examples with modern ES6+ syntax to make things concrete. We'll also use a bit of simple diagrams to visualize structure or flow, plus relatable analogies – because sometimes a good metaphor (like a **restaurant waiter** or a **power plug adapter**) makes a concept more understandable. We will also talk about common pitfalls or misuse of each pattern, so you know what to watch out for.

Our journey will start with some simple patterns and gradually work up to more sophisticated ones. By the end, you should not only understand *how* to implement these patterns in JavaScript, but also *why* they matter for crafting robust software architecture.

Understanding Design Patterns: An Essential Primer

Before we jump into exploring each design pattern one by one, it's worth spending a few minutes demystifying what design patterns really are—and why they matter to you as a developer.

Imagine you're building a piece of furniture. Over the years, carpenters have discovered that rather than reinventing the wheel each time, using a well-tested plan or "blueprint" for a chair or table not only speeds things up but yields better results. In much the same way, design patterns are proven, repeatable solutions to common problems in software design.

The Role of Patterns in Software Development

At their essence, design patterns are about **communication** and **efficiency**: - **Shared Vocabulary:** When you say "Singleton" or "Observer" in a code review or design meeting, your fellow engineers quickly understand you're talking about a common problem and solution. This shorthand builds a language that makes collaborations smoother and more effective. - **Flexibility and Maintainability:** Instead of crafting a new solution every time you face a design dilemma, patterns provide the guidance you need to structure your code in a way that makes it easier to modify and extend later. They help decouple parts of your program, so changes in one area don't inadvertently break another. - **A Tool for Problem-Solving:** Using patterns doesn't mean forcing every design into a pre-made mold. Rather, it's about choosing the right tool from your toolbox when certain challenges arise. Whether you're managing object creation, reducing interconnections between components, or dynamically extending functionality, there's a pattern that fits the task.

Common Misconceptions

You might have heard that design patterns are overly academic or "old news." In truth, the core principles behind these patterns continue to evolve along with programming languages like JavaScript. In modern development, you'll find patterns implemented using functions, closures, ES6 classes, modules, and even reactive hooks. The techniques may change, but the underlying idea—organizing solutions to recurring problems—remains as vital as ever.

Patterns vs. Frameworks

One frequent source of confusion is the relationship between patterns and frameworks. Think of a framework as a complete kitchen filled with everything needed to cook a meal. Design patterns, on the other hand, are like recipes: they offer you directions on how to best use the ingredients and tools at your disposal. Even when you work within popular frameworks (be it React, Vue, or Node.js), you're implicitly using these design patterns to structure your code.

How to Think About Patterns

Here's what to keep in mind as you progress through the book: - **Not One-Size-Fits-All:** No single design pattern is the answer to every challenge. Instead, each pattern is aimed at a particular kind of problem. Sometimes, you may use more than one in concert, or sometimes none if a more straightforward solution is more appropriate. - **A Dynamic Toolkit:** Patterns aren't static rules to follow dogmatically. They are flexible strategies that you can adapt and evolve as your project demands change. The key is understanding the *intent* behind each pattern so you can recognize when a situation calls for a particular approach. - **Hands-On Understanding:** Ultimately, patterns make more sense when seen in action. As we progress through each chapter, you'll see carefully chosen examples, some with diagrams written in text, that illustrate

3

how you can implement these patterns in JavaScript. That hands-on perspective should help bridge the gap between concept and practice.

By understanding these core ideas, you're well-equipped to appreciate the detailed discussion of each design pattern that follows. Together, we'll explore how these methods help streamline code, encourage reuse, and make software architecture more intuitive and robust.

Singleton – The One and Only

Imagine a world where, no matter how many times you try, you only ever get one instance of a particular object. That's the essence of the **Singleton pattern**. It ensures that a class has only a single instance and provides a global point of access to that instance. In other words, **there can be only one**. If you ask for that object, you either get the sole existing instance or, if none exists yet, a new one is created. But you'll never have two of them running around.

What the Singleton Solves

The Singleton is handy when you need a central, shared resource or manager that many parts of your program will use. Rather than creating new copies all over (which could lead to inconsistency), you ensure everyone uses the same one. Think about configuration settings in an application: you want all modules to read from the same config object. Or a database connection pool – you wouldn't want to create a whole new pool every time; you'd want to reuse a single one. A singleton provides a single source of truth for these scenarios.

A real-world analogy? Think of a country's government. Regardless of who is in power, there's only one official government at a time. If every piece of code in your app is like a citizen, they all refer to "the government" as a single entity. You don't get multiple governments in parallel – just one global access point (the government) that everybody knows about. (Another fun analogy: the Highlander movie quote, "There can be only one.")

When and Why to Use a Singleton

So, when would you use a Singleton? Common use cases include: - **Configuration or Settings:** As mentioned, a single configuration object that loads once and is used everywhere. - **Logging:** You typically want one logger instance writing to a file or console so that logs are centralized. - **Browser Storage or Database Access:** For example, one object managing `localStorage` or an IndexedDB connection in a web app, or a single database client in Node.js so all queries go through one instance. - **Caching:** A single in-memory cache object that different modules can check for data, to avoid duplicating caches. The reason is straightforward: you want to **avoid conflicting instances** and ensure all parts of your program refer to the same resource. It also can save resources – e.g. only one heavy object is created – and simplifies access (since any module can import or retrieve the singleton). It's like having a single coordinator or manager that everyone can use.

However, here's the thing – overusing singletons can bite you. We'll talk pitfalls in a moment, but keep in mind they introduce global state, which can make testing and debugging trickier.

How to Implement a Singleton (in JS)

In classical OOP languages, implementing a singleton often involves making a class with a private constructor and a static method to get the instance. In JavaScript, we don't have truly private constructors (aside from some newer class features), but there are simple ways to create a singleton: 1. **Module Pattern / Object Literal:** The easiest approach in JS is to use an object literal or module. If you define an object and export it (in Node or ES6 modules), every import gets the same object. Node.js actually caches required modules, so `require('mySingleton')` will always return the same instance, effectively making it a singleton by design. 2. **Closure and Factory Function:** Use an IIFE (immediately invoked function expression) or a factory function that stores an instance in a closure. Call it to get the singleton instance. If an instance already exists, it returns it; otherwise it creates it. 3. **ES6 Class with Static Instance:** Use a class with a static property that holds the one instance. The class's constructor can be designed to throw an error or return the existing instance if creation is attempted a second time. Let's look at a simple implementation using a closure (module pattern):

```javascript
// singleton.js
const ConfigSingleton = (function() {
  let instance;  // private instance

  function createInstance() {
    return {
      env: "production",
      apiKey: "12345-ABCDE",
      // ...other config settings...
    };
  }

  return {
    getInstance: function() {
      if (!instance) {
        instance = createInstance();
        console.log("Created new config instance");
      }
      return instance;
    }
  };
})();

// Usage
const configA = ConfigSingleton.getInstance();
const configB = ConfigSingleton.getInstance();
console.log(configA === configB);  // true, both
variables point to the same object
```

In this code, `ConfigSingleton` is an IIFE that returns an object with a `getInstance` method. The first time you call `getInstance()`, it creates a new config object and stores it in the `instance` variable. Subsequent calls return the same `instance`, so `configA` and `configB` end up referencing exactly the same object. We even logged a message to show that creation happens only once.

If we used an ES6 class, it could look like this:

```javascript
class SingletonLogger {
```

6

```
  constructor() {
    if (SingletonLogger._instance) {
      throw new Error("Use
SingletonLogger.getInstance() instead of new.");
    }
    SingletonLogger._instance = this;
    // ... initialization ...
  }

  log(msg) {
    console.log("[LOG]", msg);
  }

  static getInstance() {
    return SingletonLogger._instance || new
SingletonLogger();
  }
}

// Usage:
const logger1 = SingletonLogger.getInstance();
const logger2 = SingletonLogger.getInstance();
logger1.log("Hello");
console.log(logger1 === logger2); // true
```

Here we guard the constructor to prevent direct `new` after an instance exists, and provide a static `getInstance()` that either creates a new instance or returns the existing one.

Visual Diagram

```
Caller1 ----\
Caller2 -----+---> [ Singleton Instance ] (only one)
Caller3 ----/
```

No matter how many callers ask for the singleton, they all get a reference to the **same** instance. They funnel into that one object to do whatever work it provides.

Analogy Recap

We likened the singleton to a single government office. Another analogy: a singleton is like the **single player token** in a board game that all players share when it's their turn. Everyone uses that one token to indicate the current player. If someone tried to add another turn token, it would confuse the game.

Pitfalls and Misuse

Singletons can be overused. Here are some caveats: - **Global State:** A singleton is essentially a globally accessible object. Global state can lead to tight coupling; any part of your code can change it, and those changes are seen everywhere. This can make debugging a nightmare if not managed carefully. - **Testing Difficulties:** Global singletons can make unit testing harder, since tests might need to reset or mock the singleton. If one test changes the singleton's state, another test might be affected. (Solutions include resetting the singleton between tests or using dependency injection to provide a mock.) - **Hidden Dependencies:** If many modules use a singleton, it may be unclear which piece of code truly depends on it. This can make refactoring risky.
- **Concurrent Environments:** In JS we mostly have a single thread, but if you have Node.js processes or workers, each might get its own instance of a singleton module (since it's per process). That's usually fine, but just be aware it's not a single instance across separate processes. - **When Not to Use:** Don't use a singleton just to avoid passing a reference around. If two parts of code should not truly share the same instance (they just happen to create once each), a singleton could introduce unintended coupling.

Also remember that JavaScript's module system often provides singletons by default (each module is evaluated once). So in JS, you might not need a formal Singleton class – a simple module or object can suffice. Use singletons judiciously when having a single instance is logical for the design (and document that global usage clearly for your team).

Factory – Manufacturing Objects on Demand

When your code is calling `new` all over the place to create objects, it might be time to introduce a **Factory**. The Factory pattern provides an interface for creating objects in a super flexible way, without exposing the creation logic to the client. Instead of calling a constructor directly, you call a factory function or method that *spits out* the object you need. It's like ordering from a catalog: you tell the factory what kind of object you want, and it delivers it, handling all the assembly behind the scenes.

What Problem Does It Solve?

Whenever you find your code littered with `new SomeClass()` calls or big `switch`/`if` blocks deciding which subclass to instantiate, a factory can help. It **encapsulates object creation**, so that if you need to change *how* objects are created or which concrete class is returned, you can do it in one place. The Factory pattern promotes loose coupling by abstracting away the concrete types from the code that uses the objects.

A common scenario is when the exact type of object needed might depend on some configuration or environment. For instance, suppose you're writing a storage library that works in both Node and the browser. You might have a factory `createStorage()` that returns a file-system storage object for Node, but a `localStorage`-based object for the browser. The caller doesn't worry about these details – they just get an object that conforms to a known interface (say, it has `save()` and `load()` methods).

Another example: imagine a game where you can spawn different types of enemies ("Goblin", "Troll", "Dragon"). Instead of sprinkling code with `if (type==='goblin') new Goblin()` everywhere, you could have an `EnemyFactory.create(type)` that internally decides which class to instantiate. This makes the code more maintainable and extensible (add a new enemy type? Just modify the factory, not all the call sites).

When and Why to Use a Factory

Use a factory when: - **Object creation is complex** – e.g. requiring multiple steps, or assembly of parts. - **You need to decide among various classes at runtime** – as with the storage example or enemy example above.
- **You want to hide creation details from the caller** – maybe to keep the API clean or to be able to change it later without breaking code. - **Prevent tight coupling** – the code using the object shouldn't have to know about the specific classes or logic to create them.

The benefit is flexibility and cleaner code. If tomorrow the way we create an object changes (maybe we switch to a different subclass or some caching of objects), we only change the factory. The rest of the code continues calling the factory as usual. It also clarifies intent: seeing `EnemyFactory.create("dragon")` in code makes it clear we're creating an enemy, whereas `new Dragon()` exposes implementation.

How it Works

In JavaScript, factories are often just functions (or static class methods) that return an object. There are variations like **Factory Method** (where a subclass decides which object to create) and **Abstract Factory** (a factory that creates families of related objects), but let's keep it simple.

Here's a straightforward example:

```
// Factory function
function createEmployee(role, name) {
  if (role === "developer") {
    return new Developer(name);
  } else if (role === "manager") {
    return new Manager(name);
  } else {
    throw new Error("Unknown role: " + role);
  }
}

// Example classes
class Developer {
  constructor(name) {
```

```
    this.name = name;
    this.type = "developer";
  }
  sayHi() { console.log(`Hi, I'm ${this.name}, a
Developer.`); }
}
class Manager {
  constructor(name) {
    this.name = name;
    this.type = "manager";
  }
  sayHi() { console.log(`Hello, I'm ${this.name}, a
Manager.`); }
}

// Usage:
const emp1 = createEmployee("developer", "Alice");
const emp2 = createEmployee("manager", "Bob");
emp1.sayHi(); // Hi, I'm Alice, a Developer.
emp2.sayHi(); // Hello, I'm Bob, a Manager.
```

In this snippet, `createEmployee` acts as a factory. It takes a `role` and `name` and decides which class to instantiate. The calling code doesn't do `new Developer()` or `new Manager()` directly. If we added a new role "intern" later, we could extend `createEmployee` without touching the places where employees are created.

We could also use an object map to avoid the if/else:

```
const classMap = { developer: Developer, manager:
Manager };
function createEmployee(role, name) {
  const EmployeeClass = classMap[role];
  if (!EmployeeClass) throw new Error("Unknown role");
  return new EmployeeClass(name);
}
```

But the idea stands: hide those details behind a function.

Visual Diagram

```
              create()
Client --------> Factory --------> ProductA instance
                    |---------> ProductB instance
```

11

The **Client** calls `Factory.create()` (or in our case, `createEmployee("developer", ...)`). The **Factory** internally decides which **Product** type to create (Developer or Manager, etc.) and returns the appropriate instance. The client just gets an object that implements the expected interface, without caring about the exact class.

Analogy

Think of a **car factory**. You (the client) place an order for a car with certain specs. The factory knows how to build different models. You don't personally assemble the car – the factory does. You just say, "I'd like a Model S, please," and the factory handles all the complexity. If the factory changes how it builds the car (different parts or process), you wouldn't know or care; you still get a car that meets your request. Similarly, in code, you request, "Give me an object that does X," and the factory figures out the details.

Pitfalls and Considerations

- **Overuse**: If object creation is straightforward, using a factory might be overkill. Sometimes a plain constructor call is clear and sufficient. Use factories when there's clear benefit in flexibility or abstraction.
- **Indirection**: Debugging can be a tad more indirect since you need to step into the factory to see what concrete class was produced. Good naming helps mitigate this.
- **Maintenance**: The factory can become a bit complex if there are many creation paths. In such cases, consider breaking it into smaller factories or using subclassing (Factory Method pattern).
- **Parallel Class Hierarchies**: If using abstract factories, you might end up with corresponding factory classes for each product family which can be verbose. But in JS, often a single function can serve as an abstract factory by returning different types of related objects together.

In JavaScript, a lot of frameworks use factories internally. For instance, React's `React.createElement` is essentially a factory that creates React element objects (it decides what type of object to create based on input). Also, dependency injection systems in some frameworks act like abstract factories, providing you with instances of requested types.

Having set up our object "factory", let's now talk about another creational pattern that JavaScript uses at its core: the Prototype pattern.

Prototype – Cloning the Blueprint

JavaScript's object system is built on prototypes, so the **Prototype pattern** is part of its DNA. In design pattern terms, Prototype means creating new objects by copying an existing object, the prototype, rather than instantiating new ones via classes. It lets you make new instances by cloning a prototypical instance.

What Problem Does It Solve?

Sometimes you have an object and you want to make a new object that's a copy of it (perhaps with some changes). Creating a fresh object and setting it up could be expensive or complex, so instead you **clone** the existing object. The Prototype pattern is useful when: - The cost of making a new object from scratch is high (maybe it involves lots of configuration or data). - You want to avoid subclassing just to get a slightly different object. Instead, you clone a baseline object and tweak it. - You need a bunch of objects that are mostly similar to a prototype.

In classical OOP, prototype is one way to implement polymorphism without inheritance by cloning exemplars. In JavaScript, every object has an internal prototype (`proto` or via `Object.getPrototypeOf`), but here we're talking about duplicating object *data* as well, not just sharing prototypes.

When and Why to Use Prototype

- **Performance**: If object creation involves time-consuming setup, cloning an existing prepared object can be faster.
- **Simplicity**: It can simplify object creation code. Instead of repeating initialization code, have one prototypical instance and copy it.
- **Avoiding Hierarchies**: Maybe you have a complex object and multiple variants. Instead of multiple subclasses or conditionals in constructor, keep a few prototype instances (for each variant) and clone them to create new objects.
- **Dynamic object structures**: In JS, if you have an object built at runtime with certain properties, you can use that as a prototype to produce similar objects.

JavaScript supports this pattern natively via `Object.create()`. You pass it a prototype object, and it creates a new object with that prototype. Note: `Object.create(proto)` doesn't clone properties, it just sets the prototype chain, but if you combine that with property assignment you can get a cloned result.

How to Implement Prototype in JS

The simplest way is using `Object.create`. Another way is if you have a class or constructor function, you could add a method like `.clone()` that does `return Object.assign(Object.create(Object.getPrototypeOf(this)), this)` (which copies own properties to a new object with same prototype). If a deep clone is needed, you'd adjust accordingly.

Let's illustrate with an example without classes: say we have a prototype object for an enemy in a game, and we want to create multiple similar enemies quickly by cloning.

```
const enemyPrototype = {
  health: 100,
  speed: 10,
  attack(target) {
    console.log(`${this.name} attacks ${target} for
${this.damage} damage!`);
  }
};
```

```
// Create a specific enemy prototype
const goblinPrototype = Object.create(enemyPrototype);
goblinPrototype.name = "Goblin";
goblinPrototype.damage = 15;

// Now create new goblin instances by cloning the
prototype
function cloneEnemy(proto) {
  const newEnemy = Object.create(proto);
  // If we had nested objects or unique properties, we
might copy or initialize them here.
  return newEnemy;
}

const goblin1 = cloneEnemy(goblinPrototype);
const goblin2 = cloneEnemy(goblinPrototype);
goblin2.health = 80;  // each clone can have its own
state
goblin1.attack("hero"); // Goblin attacks hero for 15
damage!
goblin2.attack("hero"); // Goblin attacks hero for 15
damage!
```

Here, `enemyPrototype` is a generic template with an `attack` method. `goblinPrototype` is a specialized prototype with a name and damage. The `cloneEnemy` function uses `Object.create` to make new objects that delegate to the prototype for methods and default values. We can override properties like `health` on each instance without affecting others. We didn't have to define a Goblin class or repeat the attack method for each instance; they're all sharing from the prototype.

Alternatively, if using classes (ES6), the Prototype pattern could be as simple as creating a new instance via an existing one's data:

```
class Monster {
  constructor(name, health, damage) {
    this.name = name;
    this.health - health;
    this.damage = damage;
  }
  attack(target) {
    console.log(`${this.name} hits ${target} for
${this.damage}!`);
```

```
  }
  clone() {
    // clone this monster
    return new Monster(this.name, this.health,
this.damage);
  }
}
const ogre = new Monster("Ogre", 200, 30);
const ogre2 = ogre.clone();
```

But this is basically the same as calling the constructor again with the same data, so the pattern isn't providing a huge gain here unless object creation is more complex or involves a lot of configuration.

Visual Diagram

```
Prototype Object ---- clone() ----> New Object
                      clone() ----> Another Object
```

One **Prototype** serves as a template. Each **clone** operation makes a new object with the same structure/content (with opportunities to tweak after cloning).

Analogy

Cloning is literally the analogy. Like the famous cloning of **Dolly the sheep** – you have one sheep (object), and you create another with the same genetics (properties). You didn't go through the normal birth process (constructor), you made a copy of an existing instance.

Another analogy: using a **template document** to create new documents. Instead of starting from a blank page (which might be akin to constructing an object from scratch), you copy an existing template file and then just change what you need in the copy. You saved yourself the work of configuring all the common parts.

Pitfalls

- **Shallow vs Deep Copy**: Cloning can be tricky if your object has complex nested structures. A naive clone (like using `Object.assign` or spread `{...obj}`) makes a shallow copy – nested objects are still shared references. That could lead to weird bugs where clones are not fully independent. You may need a deep clone for truly independent copies, which is more expensive.
- **Prototype Chains**: In JS, if you use `Object.create(proto)`, the new object's prototype is the given object. That means changes to methods in the prototype reflect in all clones (which might be desired for shared behavior). However, changes to properties on the prototype affect all objects if they haven't overridden that property. Just be mindful of JS's prototypal inheritance mechanics; the design pattern doesn't require you to use `Object.create`, it could be an explicit clone function that copies everything.
- **Overuse or Misuse**: In JavaScript, since it's easy to create objects and we have garbage collection, the performance reasons to use Prototype pattern are less common. If not needed, cloning objects could add complexity or memory overhead (lots of similar objects floating around). Sometimes it's simpler to use a class or factory to generate new instances if you don't truly need clones of existing state.
- **Unique Identifiers**: If the object being cloned has some unique ID or identity in a system, cloning it might cause issues (two objects with same ID). Make sure to generate new IDs or adjust such properties post-clone to avoid conflicts.

The Prototype pattern is conceptually built into JS (as prototypal inheritance). Many libraries or frameworks leverage prototypal inheritance by creating object instances that serve as prototypes for others (like React's object model in older versions). While you might not call something "Prototype pattern" explicitly in everyday coding, understanding it helps when you want to duplicate configuration or state easily.

Now, onto a different kind of pattern: one that structures how classes work together. Our next pattern is the Adapter, a structural pattern.

Adapter – Making Incompatible Interfaces Work Together

Have you ever used a power plug adapter while traveling? Your laptop has a plug of one shape, the wall outlet is another shape, so you use an adapter in between that converts one interface to the other. In software, the **Adapter pattern** works the same way. It allows objects with incompatible interfaces to collaborate by providing a wrapper that translates between them.

What Problem Does It Solve?

Often, you have code (a class, module, or function) expecting to interact with something that has a certain interface, but you have an existing component with a different interface. Rather than modifying either the usage or the component (which might be impractical if it's from a library or heavily used elsewhere), you write an Adapter that **translates the two.

For example, suppose you have a new logging interface that expects a method `log(message)`, but you want to use an old logger that only has a function `write(msg)`. You could create `LoggerAdapter` with a `log(msg)` method that internally calls the old `write(msg)` function. Now the rest of your code can use `LoggerAdapter.log()` and under the hood it's using the old system.

Another scenario: different data formats. If one part of your system provides data as an array but another expects an object with specific keys, an adapter can take the array and output an equivalent object (or vice versa).

When and Why to Use Adapter

- **Impedance Mismatch**: Use an adapter when you want to integrate a component that doesn't directly fit the interface you need. It's common when integrating third-party or legacy code into a new system.
- **Multiple Interfaces to Standardize**: If you have several classes with similar functionality but different APIs, you might adapt them to a common interface so you can swap them easily.
- **Legacy Modernization**: Adapters can help wrap old APIs with a new interface without rewriting the old code.
- **Ease of Use**: Sometimes an adapter can provide a more convenient interface for a complex component (though that borders on Facade pattern territory; the difference is adapter is usually for compatibility, not just simplification).

The goal is **reusability and decoupling**. The code that uses the adapter doesn't need to know about the special cases of the adaptee. And the adaptee (original component) doesn't need to be changed to fit the new system. The adapter is the only place where the conversion logic lives.

How to Implement Adapter in JS

In JavaScript, an adapter is often just a class or an object that wraps another object. It implements the interface that the client expects and delegates calls to the wrapped object, possibly transforming data along the way.

Let's take a concrete example: We have a round peg and a square hole (a classic example in pattern literature). The hole expects an object with a method `fitIntoHole()`, but our round peg only has `insertIntoRoundSlot()`. We can make a `RoundPegAdapter` with a `fitIntoHole()` that internally calls the peg's `insertIntoRoundSlot()`.

For a more real example, consider adapting an old payment system to a new interface:

```
// Old payment system (adaptee)
```

```javascript
const OldPaymentSystem = {
  processPayment(amount, currency) {
    console.log(`Processed payment of ${amount}
${currency} via OLD system.`);
  }
};

// New expected interface for payments (target
interface)
class PaymentProcessor {
  constructor() {
    this.currency = "USD";
  }
  pay(amount) {
    // Internally use the old system
    OldPaymentSystem.processPayment(amount,
this.currency);
  }
}

// Usage:
const payment = new PaymentProcessor();
payment.pay(100);
// Output: Processed payment of 100 USD via OLD system.
```

Here, `PaymentProcessor` is an adapter that wraps the old system. The new code expects to call `pay(amount)` on an object. The adapter provides that, and inside it calls the old system's `processPayment(amount, currency)`. We even set a default currency in the adapter to keep the interface simple.

Another simple form: if just one function is mismatched, an adapter can be a function:

```javascript
// Old function we want to use
function oldLog(msg) {
  console.log("OLD LOG:", msg);
}

// New code expects a logger with .log()
const newLogger = {
  log(message) {
    // adapt to old interface
    oldLog(message);
  }
```

```
};

// Usage:
newLogger.log("Hello");
// Output: OLD LOG: Hello
```

Now `newLogger` fits the expected interface (has a `.log` method), but it uses `oldLog` internally.

Visual Diagram

```
Client ---> [Adapter] ---> Adaptee
```

The **Client** calls the **Adapter** using the interface it expects. The **Adapter** translates that into one or more calls to the **Adaptee** (the existing component with a different interface), and possibly returns a result back to the client in the format it expects.

If we expand it conceptually: - **Target interface**: what the client expects (e.g., a `pay()` method). - **Adaptee interface**: what the wrapped object provides (e.g., `processPayment()`). - The adapter implements the target interface and holds an instance of the adaptee. Its methods call adaptee's methods.

Analogy

Besides the power plug adapter (which is the namesake analogy), another analogy is a **language translator**. Imagine you speak English and you're at a meeting with a person who speaks Japanese, and neither of you speaks the other's language. A translator who knows both languages acts as an adapter. You speak English to the translator (target interface), the translator translates to Japanese and speaks to the other person (adaptee interface), and then translates the Japanese response back to English for you. The translator doesn't change the content of the conversation, just the form so each side can understand.

Similarly, an adapter in code changes the form of calls or data between two parts so they can work together.

Pitfalls

- **Added Complexity**: It's an extra layer of indirection. In some cases, if you control both sides of the code, it might be simpler to just change one side to match the other. Adapters are most valuable when that's not feasible.
- **Performance**: Usually negligible overhead (just a simple wrapper call), but if an adapter needs to transform a lot of data or is in a hot code path called thousands of times, be mindful of the cost.
- **Maintenance**: The adapter needs to be updated if either the client's expected interface or the adaptee's interface changes. It's a piece ofcan fall out of sync if not maintained. Good tests around adapters can catch mismatches.
- **Overuse**: If you find yourself writing a lot of adapters, maybe the interfaces of your subsystems need reconsideration. Adapters are a workaround for mismatch; too many might indicate a bigger design issue.
- **Alternative**: Sometimes the Observer or Mediator patterns can be used if the mismatch is about event handling or communication rather than method signatures.

Adapters are very common in real-world code. For instance, many Node.js callback-based libraries have Promise-based adapter wrappers created by the community (to adapt from callback style to Promise style). Or when using a library that doesn't quite match what you need, you write a small wrapper (adapter) to make it fit your usage. Even React has adapters for its test utils (like Enzyme's adapter for different React versions) to bridge differences.

Moving on, let's discuss the Facade pattern, which also provides an interface but with a different intent.

Facade – A Simplified Interface to a Complex System

"Could you dumb it down for me?" – If a system could talk, it would ask for a **Facade** when things get overly complex. The Facade pattern provides a simplified, high-level interface to a complex subsystem or set of classes. Instead of interacting with lots of intricate parts, you interact with one easy-to-use object that internally coordinates all those parts.

What Problem Does It Solve?

Large systems often have many classes or components that need to work together. Without a facade, an outsider would have to directly call multiple methods in the right order and manage a lot of details. A Facade solves the problem of **too much complexity exposed**. It presents a clean, one-stop interface for common operations, hiding the inner workings.

For example, consider a home theater system with a TV, DVD player, speakers, and lights. To "watch a movie" you might have to: turn on the TV, switch TV to the DVD input, turn on the DVD player, insert a disc, press play, dim the lights, and so on. Without a facade, any code that wants to initiate "movie mode" has to do all that. With a Facade object, say `HomeTheaterFacade`, you could have a single method `watchMovie(title)` that internally does all those steps. The client code then just calls `homeTheater.watchMovie("Inception")` and relaxes.

Another example: interacting with a complex library (maybe a library for image processing that requires creating many objects and calling them in sequence to apply a filter). A Facade could wrap those steps into a simple function like `applyOldPhotoFilter(image)` that internally sets up all the needed objects and calls them. The user of the Facade doesn't need to manage the details.

When and why use a Facade

- **Simplify usage**: When you have a complex API or set of interfaces that most clients use in standard ways, provide a facade to simplify those common tasks.
- **Prevent tight coupling to subsystems**: Clients don't need to know the details of the subsystem classes. They only talk to the facade. This decouples client code from the specifics of the subsystem, which could change behind the facade without affecting the client.
- **Multiple subsystems or layers**: In layered architectures, a facade can provide a simple interface to the functionality of an entire layer. For example, a single class that provides easy methods for the UI layer to use the business logic layer without exposing all of its classes.
- **Improving readability**: Code that says `userService.registerUser(name, email)` is clearer than code that inlines all the steps to create user, send welcome email, set default preferences, etc. The facade `registerUser` method can do all that behind the scenes.

Essentially, use a facade when you want to provide a *simplified view* of a chunk of functionality. It's like giving someone a remote control instead of asking them to manually operate each part of the TV, sound system, etc.

How to Implement Facade in JS

A facade can just be a set of functions or a class with methods that abstract away complex sequences of calls. The facade holds references to the necessary subsystems and knows how to coordinate them.

Let's create a small example: a `ComputerFacade` that starts up a computer. Internally, suppose we have to: - Power on the CPU. - Check the BIOS. - Load the bootloader from disk into memory. - Start the operating system.

Without facade, a client would need to call the CPU, BIOS, Disk, and Memory components in sequence correctly. With facade:

```javascript
// Subsystem components (simulated)
class CPU {
  start() { console.log("CPU started"); }
}

class Memory {
  load(address, data) { console.log(`Loaded data into
memory at ${address}`); }
}

class HardDrive {
  read(sector, size) {
    console.log(`Read ${size} bytes from sector
${sector}`);
    return "bootloader";  // dummy data
  }
}

// Facade
class ComputerFacade {
  constructor() {
    this.cpu = new CPU();
    this.memory = new Memory();
    this.hd = new HardDrive();
  }

  startComputer() {
    console.log("Starting computer...");
    const bootData = this.hd.read(0, 512);
    this.memory.load(0, bootData);
    this.cpu.start();
    console.log("Computer started.");
  }
}

// Usage:
const computer = new ComputerFacade();
computer.startComputer();
// Output:
// Starting computer...
// Read 512 bytes from sector 0
// Loaded data into memory at 0
// CPU started
// Computer started.
```

The ComputerFacade **provides a simple** startComputer() **method.
The client doesn't need to know about disk sectors or memory**

addresses or CPU opcodes. They just call `startComputer()`.
Internally, the facade orchestrates the calls to the hard drive,
memory, and CPU in the correct order.

Another web dev example: consider a library like jQuery. jQuery
can be thought of as a Facade over the DOM and XHR and other
browser APIs. Instead of having to call
`document.querySelectorAll`, `element.addEventListener`,
`XMLHttpRequest` or `fetch`, etc., you could just do
`$(".btn").hide()` or `$.get("/api/data")`. That single call might
internally use several DOM or network operations. The user of
jQuery doesn't need to manage those directly.

Visual Diagram

Without Facade:

```
Client -> [Subsystem A]
Client -> [Subsystem B]
Client -> [Subsystem C]
```

The client directly calls multiple subsystems (and thus needs detailed
knowledge of each).

With Facade:

```
Client -> [ Facade ] -> Subsystem A
                  \-> Subsystem B
                  \-> Subsystem C
```

The **Client** talks to a single **Facade**. The Facade then talks to the
necessary subsystems. The client is simplified, and subsystem
complexity is hidden behind the facade.

Analogy

We already used the **home theater remote** analogy. Another:
restaurant waiter. In a restaurant, if you want a meal, you (client)
don't go to the chef, the ingredient pantry, and the stove yourself.
You just tell the waiter (facade) what you want from the menu. The

waiter translates that into kitchen operations: they place the order with the kitchen, maybe coordinate with the bartender for your drink, etc., then deliver everything to you. From your perspective, you had a simple interface (the menu and a single person to talk to) for a complex operation (cooking a meal).

Similarly, a facade offers a simple menu of operations, and handles the gritty details internally.

Pitfalls

- **Limited functionality**: A facade typically doesn't expose every capability of the underlying system, by design (it's simplified). If a client needs something not supported by the facade, they might have to bypass it and use the subsystem directly. That's fine – facade is for convenience, not an exclusive access point.
- **Performance**: If the facade does a lot under the hood, a client might inadvertently do more work than they realize by calling a simple-looking method. For example, `facade.generateReport()` might be doing tons of data crunching – which is okay, but the interface doesn't telegraph the cost. This isn't really a pitfall of facade per se, just something to document if needed.
- **Over-simplification**: If you make the facade too simple, you might not expose some useful features. If you make it too complex, it might defeat the purpose. It's a balance. Ideally, the facade covers the 80% common use cases easily, and for the other 20% the clients can drop down to the detailed API if needed.
- **Maintenance**: The facade needs to be updated when subsystems change or when new common operations need to be supported. It's an extra layer to maintain. However, that maintenance is usually easier than maintaining many places where the complex logic would have been otherwise.

In JavaScript, you'll find facades in many libraries (providing simpler APIs for complex browser features). For instance, many animation libraries provide a facade for `requestAnimationFrame`, timeline management, etc., so you can just call a simple function to animate something instead of juggling all the details.

Now, let's move to the Decorator pattern, which deals with dynamically extending behavior.

Decorator – Adding Functionality Without Subclassing

Say you have an object and you want to give it some new abilities, but you don't want to alter its original code or create a bunch of subclasses for every combination of features. The **Decorator pattern** lets you "wrap" an object with another object to extend its behavior at runtime. This provides a flexible alternative to subclassing for extending functionality.

What Problem Does It Solve?

The typical scenario: You have a core class, and various optional features that can be added. If you tried to account for every combination with subclasses, it would explode in number. For example, a basic `Car` class and optional features like sunroof, spoiler, sports rims, navigation. If you made subclasses for combinations, you'd have `CarWithSunroof`, `CarWithSpoiler`, `CarWithSunroofSpoiler`, `CarWithSpoilerRimsNav`, and so on — a combinatorial explosion. Instead, Decorator pattern says: design your `Car` class and then create decorator classes for each feature. You can wrap a `Car` in a `SunroofDecorator` to add sunroof behavior, wrap that in a `SpoilerDecorator` to add a spoiler, etc. Each decorator adds its own part and delegates the rest.

Each decorator implements the same interface as the object it decorates (so it can stand in for it) and contains a reference to the object it's decorating. It forwards calls to the original object (so it behaves like the original) but can also add to the behavior either before or after delegating.

When and Why to Use Decorator

- **Extending objects dynamically**: When you want to add responsibilities to individual objects, not to all objects of a class, and do so without altering the class itself.
- **Avoid subclass explosion**: When using inheritance for adding features leads to too many subclasses. Decorators let you add features with composition instead of inheritance, and mix and match them as needed.
- **Pluggable features**: Think of a web server where you can add logging, authentication, compression, etc., around a base request handler. Middleware in Node's Express or Koa is conceptually similar to a decorator chain: each middleware wraps the core behavior and adds something.
- **Transparent augmentation**: Ideally, decorators adhere to the same interface as the component they wrap, so from the outside you can treat a decorated object the same as an undecorated one (aside from the new features). This transparency means you can write code that works with the base interface, and it can also handle decorated versions.

Why use it: It gives flexibility. You can start with a simple object and layer on extras as needed, even at runtime. You can also remove them or change them dynamically. Each decorator focpiece of functionality (Single Responsibility Principle), and you can combine them without creating a subclass for each combination.

How to Implement Decorator in JS

A decorator in JS can be a class that takes an object in its constructor and implements the same interface by delegating to that object and adding something. Or it can be done with function wrappers if we're dealing with functions.

Let's demonstrate with the classic coffee example (often used in pattern explanations):

We have `Coffee` interface with `getCost()` and `getDescription()`. A `SimpleCoffee` provides base cost and description. We then have decorators: `MilkDecorator`, `SugarDecorator` that wrap a coffee and add to its cost/description.

```
// Component interface
class Coffee {
  getCost() { return 0; }
  getDescription() { return ""; }
}

// Concrete component
class SimpleCoffee extends Coffee {
  getCost() {
    return 5;
  }

  getDescription() {
    return "Plain Coffee";
  }
}

// Base Decorator class (optional, to enforce
interface)
class CoffeeDecorator extends Coffee {
  constructor(coffee) {
    super();
    this.coffee = coffee;
  }

  getCost() {
    return this.coffee.getCost();
  }

  getDescription() {
    return this.coffee.getDescription();
  }
}

// Concrete Decorators
class MilkDecorator extends CoffeeDecorator {
  getCost() {
    return super.getCost() + 1;
  }

  getDescription() {
```

```
      return super.getDescription() + ", with Milk";
  }
}
class SugarDecorator extends CoffeeDecorator {
  getCost() {
    return super.getCost() + 0.5;
  }

  getDescription() {
    return super.getDescription() + ", with Sugar";
  }
}

// Usage:
let myCoffee = new SimpleCoffee();
console.log(myCoffee.getDescription(), "$" +
myCoffee.getCost());
// Plain Coffee $5

myCoffee = new MilkDecorator(myCoffee);
myCoffee = new SugarDecorator(myCoffee);
console.log(myCoffee.getDescription(), "$" +
myCoffee.getCost());
// Plain Coffee, with Milk, with Sugar $6.5
```

We started with a `SimpleCoffee` (cost $5). Then wrapped it in `MilkDecorator`, which adds $1 and appends to description. Then wrapped that in `SugarDecorator`, adding $0.5. Each decorator took in the previous object and now our `myCoffee` variable references the outermost decorator, but from the outside it's still a `Coffee`: it has `getCost` and `getDescription`. When we call those, the calls go through the decorators to the inner object.

The line `super.getCost()` in `MilkDecorator` calls `CoffeeDecorator.getCost`, which returns `this.coffee.getCost()`. That ends up calling the wrapped object's cost (which could be another decorator or the SimpleCoffee). This cascading continues until it hits the SimpleCoffee's `getCost`.

Another example using functions (for a simpler case like logging):

```
function addLogging(fn) {
  return function(...args) {
    console.log(`Calling ${fn.name} with`, args);
```

```
    const result = fn.apply(this, args);
    console.log(`${fn.name} returned`, result);
    return result;
  };
}

function multiply(a, b) {
  return a * b;
}

const multiplyWithLogging = addLogging(multiply);
multiplyWithLogging(2, 3);
// Logs: "Calling multiply with [2,3]"
//       "multiply returned 6"
// Returns 6
```

Here `addLogging` is a decorator function that wraps any function `fn` with additional logging behavior. We didn't change `multiply` itself or make a subclass of it (that doesn't make sense for functions, but you get the idea). We created a new function that adds logs and then calls the original.

This is often how we decorate functions in JS (like adding event throttling, caching, etc., by wrapping in another function).

TypeScript also supports a decorator syntax for classes and methods (e.g., `@readonly` decorator on a property), which at runtime actually wraps or modifies the class. Those are basically compiler-assisted decorator patterns.

Visual Diagram

```
              +-------------------+
Client ---->| Decorator B       |
            |   +------------+ |
            |   | Decorator A| |
            |   |   +--------+ |
            |   |   | Object | |
            |   |   +--------+ |
            |   +------------+ |
            +-------------------+

(Client calls ->) DecoratorB.getCost() ----->
DecoratorA.getCost() -----> Object.getCost()
```

Think of it like layers of an onion. The **Client** calls a method on the outermost **Decorator** (B). Decorator B might add something, then call the same method on Decorator A. Decorator A adds something, then calls the method on the core **Object**. The result then bubbles back out: Object returns base cost, A adds to it, returns to B, B adds to it, returns to client.

If multiple methods are decorated, each follows a similar pattern.

Another simpler depiction:

```
BaseComponent -> DecoratorA -> DecoratorB
```

Chaining from right (component) to left (client sees DecoratorB, which wraps A, which wraps component).

Analogy

One popular analogy: **Christmas tree decorations**. You have a plain tree (the core object). Then you put on lights (decorator) which add blinking behavior. Then you put on ornaments (decorator) which add color spots. Then tinsel (another decorator). Each addition changes the appearance of the tree, but the tree is still fundamentally a tree. You didn't create a whole new kind of tree; you just decorated an existing one dynamically. Also, you could remove an ornament or add another without affecting the tree itself or needing a special Tree subclass.

Another analogy: **Layers of clothing**. You (the person, core object) put on a jacket (decorator) to add pockets and warmth, then put on a reflective vest (another decorator) to add visibility at night. You still walk and talk like the same person (interface unchanged), but now you have extra features (carrying items, being seen in the dark). If you get too hot, you can remove the jacket (remove that decorator) at runtime.

Pitfalls

- **Many Small Objects**: Decorators result in a lot of objects wrapping each other. If you have a heavily decorated object, debugging or understanding the call sequence can be complicated. It can also use more memory due to multiple wrapper objects, though usually that's not a big issue.
- **Order Matters**: If you apply decorators in a different order, you might get a different outcome or performance. For example, if one decorator buffers output and another encrypts it, doing one before the other yields different results. Usually you control the order, but it's something to document.
- **Object Identity**: The final wrapped object is not the same instance as the core object. If code checks for specific types with `instanceof`, it might not see through the decoration (unless decorators subclass the same base class). In our coffee example, after decorating, `myCoffee instanceof SimpleCoffee` is false. This is typically fine because we treat everything as `Coffee`, but it's worth noting.
- **Transparency vs. Leaky Abstraction**: If the client or other parts of code start to be aware of the decorators (like trying to unwrap them or call methods specific to a decorator), it breaks the pattern's benefit. Ideally, outside code should use the core interface only.
- **Alternate Solutions**: Sometimes using mixins or the Strategy pattern or even just configuration options can avoid the need for decorators. Decorator is most useful when you need the ability to add/remove features at runtime or have lots of optional features to combine.

In modern JS, we see the decorator pattern (or something similar to it) in: - React's older **Higher-Order Components (HOC)**, which essentially wrap a component with additional functionality (though now hooks are more common). - Express middleware: every middleware adds functionality and calls `next()`, wrapping the core request handling. - Redux store enhancers can be thought of as decorators for the store (they wrap the store's dispatch function to add logging, etc.). - Function decorators like the `addLogging` example are common utility patterns. - And of course, any time you manually wrap an object to add features, you're doing a decorator-like thing.

Now, on to the Proxy pattern, which might sound similar since it also involves wrapping an object, but for different reasons.

Proxy – The Object Stand-in (The Middleman)

The **Proxy pattern** provides a surrogate or placeholder for another object, controlling access to it. The proxy acts on behalf of the real object (which we often call the *real subject* or *wrapped object*). It has the same interface as the real object, so clients can use it interchangeably, but the proxy adds an extra layer of behavior.

What Problem Does It Solve?

Proxies are versatile. They solve problems such as: - **Lazy Initialization (Virtual Proxy):** If an object is expensive to create or load (e.g., it involves disk I/O or heavy computation), a proxy can be used to delay that creation until it's absolutely needed. The proxy stands in and loads/creates the real object when a method is first called on it. - **Access Control (Protection Proxy):** If you want to control access to an object (for example, allow only certain users to call certain methods, or prevent modifications), a proxy can perform checks before delegating to the real object. - **Logging or Auditing (Logging Proxy):** A proxy can log every call that goes through to the real object, which is useful for debugging or audit trails. - **Remote Proxy:** In distributed systems, a local proxy object represents a remote object (like a stub in RPC). The proxy handles the communication details (serialization, network calls) to talk to the real object elsewhere. To the client, it looks like a local object with the same methods. - **Smart Reference:** The proxy might manage additional actions when an object is accessed. For example, reference counting (to delete the object when no one is using it), or loading additional data on the fly, or synchronizing concurrent access.

In summary, proxies control and mediate access to an object. Unlike a decorator, the proxy's goal is not to add new *domain* behavior, but to enforce or add *administrative* or *structural* behavior (like access control, lazy loading, etc.) while keeping the interface intact.

JavaScript in particular has a powerful `Proxy` object (with capital P) introduced in ES6 that allows you to intercept low-level operations on objects (like property access, assignment, enumeration, function calls, etc.). That is essentially a language-level hook for implementing the Proxy pattern in a very general way.

When and Why to Use Proxy

- **Lazy loading**: Use a proxy when you want to defer the creation/loading of an object. This is common for things like loading large images, objects that represent data from a database, etc. The proxy creates the real object only when you actually need it.
- **Access control**: When certain actions on an object should be restricted, or usage should be monitored, a proxy can handle that. For example, an object that handles a file might have a proxy that checks if the file is locked before allowing write operations.
- **Logging/monitoring**: If you want to track usage of an object (say count how many times methods are called, or log every access for debugging), a proxy can do that transparently to the client and real object.
- **Performance enhancements**: A proxy could cache results of expensive operations from the real object and serve them if the same request comes again (acting like a cache proxy).
- **Distributed systems**: If you have objects in another context (like WebWorkers, or server side), a proxy can abstract the remote calls. In Node, for instance, you could have a proxy object that actually sends messages to a child process or to a web service.

The key difference from some other patterns: the client typically is not aware that it's using a proxy; it just sees the interface it expects.

The proxy either eventually calls the real object or in some cases might entirely handle the request itself (like caching or short-circuiting with an access denied error).

How to Implement

We have two main ways: manually writing a class that wraps another object (similar to how we did decorator, but the intent is different), or using ES6 `Proxy`.

Manual Proxy Example (Protection Proxy): Suppose we have a `BankAccount` class. We want a proxy that limits withdrawals to a certain amount to protect the account.

```
class BankAccount {
  constructor(initialBalance) {
    this.balance = initialBalance;
  }

  deposit(amount) {
    this.balance += amount;
    console.log(`Deposited $${amount}. Balance:
$${this.balance}`);
  }

  withdraw(amount) {
    if (amount > this.balance) {
      console.log("Insufficient funds!");
      return false;
    }

    this.balance -= amount;
    console.log(`Withdrew $${amount}. Balance:
$${this.balance}`);
    return true;
  }
}

// Proxy that limits withdrawals to $100 at a time.
class BankAccountProxy {
  constructor(realAccount) {
    this.realAccount = realAccount;
  }
```

```
  deposit(amount) {
    return this.realAccount.deposit(amount);
  }

  withdraw(amount) {
    if (amount > 100) {
      console.log("Withdrawal blocked: over $100
limit.");
      return false;
    }

    return this.realAccount.withdraw(amount);
  }
}

// Usage:
const account = new BankAccount(500);
const proxyAccount = new BankAccountProxy(account);

proxyAccount.deposit(50);    // Deposited $50. Balance:
$550
proxyAccount.withdraw(120); // Withdrawal blocked: over
$100 limit.
proxyAccount.withdraw(80);   // Withdrew $80. Balance:
$470
```

Here, `BankAccountProxy` looks just like a `BankAccount` to the client (same methods). It delegates deposit directly, but for withdraw it adds a check (ensuring the amount is not over 100) before calling the real account's withdraw. The client could use `proxyAccount` interchangeably with a `BankAccount` instance for deposit/withdraw operations.

Using ES6 Proxy for a Virtual Proxy (Lazy Initialization): Now, let's say we have an object that represents a large image. We don't want to load the image data into memory until someone actually tries to access it (maybe calls a `display()` method or gets its data).

We can use JavaScript's `Proxy` to intercept property access:

```
function createImageProxy(filename) {
  let realImage = null;
  return new Proxy({}, {
    get(target, prop) {
```

```
      if (prop === 'display') {
        // If display is called, ensure realImage is
loaded, then call its display
        return function() {
          if (!realImage) {
            console.log("Loading image from disk...");
            realImage = {
              filename: filename,
              display() { console.log(`Displaying
${this.filename}`); }
            };
          }

          realImage.display();
        };
      } else {
        // For any other properties, if needed, load
realImage first, then return property.
        if (!realImage) {
          console.log("Loading image from disk...");
          realImage = {
            filename: filename,
            display() { console.log(`Displaying
${this.filename}`); }
          };
        }

        return realImage[prop];
      }
    }
  });
}

// Usage:
const image = createImageProxy("photo.png");
// At this point, image is a proxy, real image not
loaded yet.
console.log("About to display image...");
image.display();
// Output: Loading image from disk...
//         Displaying photo.png
image.display();
// Output: Displaying photo.png (no loading this time,
already loaded)
```

Here, `createImageProxy` returns a Proxy object. The proxy's `get` trap intercepts property access. If the `display` method is accessed, it lazily loads the real image (simulated by an object with display method) and then calls it. The first time we call `image.display()`, it logs "Loading image from disk..." (simulating the heavy operation) then "Displaying photo.png". The second time, it sees `realImage` is already there, so it just calls display without loading again.

This is a simplistic example, but it shows how a proxy can control access. The client just knows it has an object with a `display()` method. It doesn't know that behind the scenes the actual image was only loaded at the last moment.

Visual Diagram

```
Client --> Proxy --> RealSubject
```

The **Client** calls methods on the **Proxy** exactly as it would on the **RealSubject**. The **Proxy** decides how and when to pass the request to the RealSubject. Sometimes the proxy creates the RealSubject on the fly, or checks conditions, or modifies parameters, etc., before forwarding.

If you had multiple clients, they all go through the same proxy, which might for example ensure only one real subject is created or enforce shared logging etc.

Analogy

A good analogy from earlier: a **personal assistant** screening calls for a boss. If you call the boss's number, you might reach the assistant (proxy). The assistant can handle some tasks without bothering the boss (e.g., "The boss is out, can I take a message?" or schedule a meeting). If it's something important, the assistant will forward the call to the boss (real subject). From your perspective as the caller (client), you dialed one number (interface same as calling boss directly), but your request went through a gatekeeper. The assistant acts as a protection proxy (screening calls) and a virtual proxy (only bothering the boss if needed).

Another analogy: **Online banking ATM**. When you check your bank balance at an ATM (client to ATM's bank interface), the ATM is like a proxy for the bank's central system. It might cache your balance after fetching it the first time (so the second time it displays quickly without asking the central system again, acting as a caching proxy). It might enforce limits on withdrawal (protection proxy), etc., before actually sending the request to the bank's server.

Pitfalls

- **Added latency**: A proxy adds a little overhead (an extra method call or check). Usually trivial, but if performance is critical or the extra logic is heavy, it could matter. For example, heavy logging on every call might slow things.
- **Complexity**: It's another piece to manage. Overusing proxies can make the system harder to understand because you have to know about that intermediate layer. If something doesn't work, you have to consider: is the proxy blocking it?
- **Transparency vs. Breaking Interface**: A well-implemented proxy doesn't change the interface or semantics of the real object's methods (unless intentionally blocking). But a poorly implemented one might, for example, not perfectly mimic some behavior (maybe it doesn't forward all properties, etc.). The ES6 Proxy is powerful but also easy to misuse because you have to handle all traps properly to truly mimic an object.
- **Debugging**: Stack traces might show proxy handlers, which could confuse debugging if you're not aware of them. Also, if the proxy hides the fact that something wasn't done (like lazy loading not happening until later), it might be a bit tricky to trace when certain initialization happened.
- **Security**: Ironically, while proxies can add security, if someone can bypass the proxy and get direct access to the real object (maybe through some reference leak), then all those checks can be circumvented. So you have to ensure the real object isn't accessible except via the proxy if protection is the goal.

ES6 Proxy in JavaScript has some gotchas. For instance, using a Proxy on large objects can break optimizations in the JS engine. Also, certain built-in operations aren't trap-able (like equality checks or `instanceof` you have to handle carefully). But for many uses (like Vue.js reactivity uses proxies to detect changes), it's extremely powerful.

Alright, we've covered many structural patterns. Now let's jump into the behavioral patterns, starting with one you likely use often: the Observer pattern.

Observer – Keeping Objects in the Loop

The **Observer pattern** defines a one-to-many dependency between objects so that when one object (the subject) changes state, all its dependents (observers) are notified and can update automatically. It's the backbone of event-driven programming: an object (subject) maintains a list of observers, and when something interesting happens, it notifies them.

What Problem Does It Solve?

The need for components to **react to changes or events** in other components without being tightly coupled. Instead of object A having to know about and call methods on objects B, C, and D when something happens, A simply broadcasts an event or message. Then B, C, and D, if they are interested, will have subscribed to these events and will react. A (the subject) doesn't need to know who is listening, and B/C/D (the observers) don't need to know about A's internal details – just that it will notify them.

In JavaScript, this pattern is everywhere: - **DOM events:** e.g., a button (subject) emits a "click" event, and multiple listeners (observers) can be attached to handle that. - **Node.js EventEmitter:** many Node classes (like streams or servers) allow observers to `.on('eventName', callback)` to get notified of events. - **Pub/Sub systems:** libraries or patterns where one part of the app emits events (like `'userLoggedIn'`) and others listen. - **Front-end frameworks:**

Angular's EventEmitter, Vue's reactive watchers, React's state change triggers re-render (which is a form of observer under the hood). - **Model-View synchronization:** In classic MVC, the model is the subject and the views are observers; when the model changes, it notifies views to update.

So the problem it solves is **decoupling** the object that has the data/does something from the objects that want to know about it. It's a way to broadcast info without hardcoding receivers.

When and Why to Use Observer

- **Event handling:** Whenever something of interest happens in one part of your system that other parts should know about. Instead of polling or tight coupling, observer lets the interested parts register and be called.
- **Cross-component communication:** In complex UIs, one component's action might affect others (e.g., selecting an item in a list should update details view). Using observer (or pub/sub), you can have the components communicate indirectly through events.
- **Dynamic relationships:** Observers can be added or removed at runtime. So if a new object comes along that needs to know about events, it just subscribes. The subject's code doesn't change.
- **Multicast distribution:** One subject, many targets. This is more efficient and cleaner than the subject calling each target individually (and knowing about them).

Why: It **promotes loose coupling and scalability**. Observers and subjects can vary independently. You can have zero, one, or many observers for a subject without altering the subject. Observers can handle events in different ways without the subject caring. It's very flexible — you can even change what gets observed or who observes on the fly.

How to Implement Observer in JS

The typical setup: - A **Subject** class that has methods to subscribe (attach an observer), unsubscribe (detach), and notify (which calls all observers). - Observers can be simple functions (especially in JS, we often use callbacks) or objects with a specific update method.

Let's implement a simple Subject:

```
class Subject {
  constructor() {
    this.observers = [];
  }

  subscribe(fn) {
    this.observers.push(fn);
  }

  unsubscribe(fn) {
    this.observers = this.observers.filter(observer =>
observer !== fn);
  }

  notify(data) {
    this.observers.forEach(observer => observer(data));
  }
}

// Example usage:
const newsletter = new Subject();

function bobSubscriber(article) {
  console.log("Bob sees new article:", article.title);
}

function aliceSubscriber(article) {
  console.log("Alice sees new article:",
article.title);
}

newsletter.subscribe(bobSubscriber);
newsletter.subscribe(aliceSubscriber);

// Later when a new article is published:
newsletter.notify({ title: "Design Patterns in JS",
content: "..." });
// Bob sees new article: Design Patterns in JS
// Alice sees new article: Design Patterns in JS
```

```
newsletter.unsubscribe(bobSubscriber);

// Another notification
newsletter.notify({ title: "Observer Pattern
Explained", content: "..." });
// Alice sees new article: Observer Pattern Explained
```

In this code, `Subject` maintains an array of observers (in this case, functions that take some data). `subscribe` adds a function to the list. `unsubscribe` removes it. `notify` goes through the list and calls each function, passing along some data (here, an article object).

We used functions as observers for simplicity. We could also define an `Observer` class with an `update()` method and have subjects call `observer.update(data)`, but in JS that's not necessary unless you want formal structure.

Node.js's built-in EventEmitter works similarly but with support for

```
const EventEmitter = require('events');
const newsletterEmitter = new EventEmitter();

newsletterEmitter.on('new-article', bobSubscriber);
newsletterEmitter.on('new-article', aliceSubscriber);

// When event occurs:
newsletterEmitter.emit('new-article', { title:
"Something", content: "..." });
```

This allows multiple event types on one subject.

Visual Diagram

```
        /--> Observer1
Subject ----> Observer2
        \--> Observer3
```

One **Subject** (publisher) to many **Observers** (subscribers). When the subject's state changes or an event happens, it calls each observer. The observers had previously registered interest.

Usually, the subject would have something like `observers: []`. Observers register via `subscribe`, and the subject calls them on `notify` or when an internal event triggers.

Analogy

A classic analogy: **magazine subscription**. A magazine publisher (subject) prints issues. Readers can subscribe (give their address to the publisher). Whenever a new issue is out, the publisher sends it to all subscribers (notify). If a subscriber no longer wants it, they unsubscribe (remove from list). The publisher doesn't individually call each reader to discuss content; they just send out the magazines. And readers don't have to call the publisher to ask "is there a new issue?" – it arrives automatically, which is more efficient.

Another: **YouTube channel notifications**. You subscribe to a channel (subject). When the creator uploads a new video, YouTube sends notifications to all subscribers. The creator (subject) doesn't directly notify you; YouTube's system does it once triggered.

Also, **event organizers and attendees**: If you RSVP to an event (subscribe to updates), if the event details change (time or venue), the organizer might send out an email to all RSVP'd attendees informing them. If you didn't RSVP, you wouldn't get the update.

Pitfalls

- If an observer is long-lived and a subject goes away (or vice versa), you must unsubscribe appropriately. In browsers, forgetting to remove event listeners can cause memory leaks because the DOM element might not get garbage-collected if listeners still reference it.
- **Unexpected updates**: Observers need to be prepared to handle updates at any time. If the subject notifies at a time that an observer isn't expecting (like maybe in the middle of some operation), it could cause issues. Sometimes you buffer notifications or schedule them at safe times.

- **Order of notifications**: Usually, the order observers are notified is not guaranteed (or is the order of subscription). If two observers have a dependency on each other, relying on notification order can be problematic.
- **Performance**: Notifying a lot of observers can be slow if done too frequently. For example, if a subject is updated in a tight loop and notifies each time, and you have 100 observers, that could be costly. A solution is coalescing changes or only notifying when a significant change happens.
- **Too many updates (thrashing)**: Observers might trigger updates to subjects or other observers, causing cascades. You have to be careful to avoid infinite loops (e.g., Observer A, when notified, changes Subject which triggers another notify, etc. – one should detect and avoid such cycles).
- **Weak references**: In some languages, holding strong references to observers can prevent them from being garbage collected. JavaScript doesn't have built-in weak references in EventEmitter, but now we have `WeakRef` and stuff, although rarely used in this scenario. More commonly, you explicitly unsubscribe to break the reference.

Despite pitfalls, Observer is extremely useful. Patterns like Model-View-Controller (MVC) rely on it: models notify views of changes. In modern frameworks: React's useEffect kind of sets up an observer for props/state changes, Vue watchers observe data changes, etc.

Alright, our next pattern is Strategy, which helps us swap out algorithms easily.

Strategy – Different Ways to Do the Same Thing

The **Strategy pattern** allows you to define a family of algorithms, encapsulate each one as a separate "strategy" class (or function), and make them interchangeable from the context's perspective. The context object can switch strategies or have one injected, and it will use that strategy without needing to know the details. This pattern is also known as the **Policy** pattern in some contexts.

What Problem Does It Solve?

When you have multiple ways of accomplishing a task and you want to choose among them dynamically or easily change which one you use. Without strategy, you might write something like:

```
if (algorithmType === 'A') {
  // do it one way
} else if (algorithmType === 'B') {
  // do it another way
}
```

This is okay for two ways, but if you have many or if you want to be able to add more without modifying this code, it gets messy. Also, the code for each algorithm might be lengthy, making this function huge.

Strategy pattern says: define each algorithm in its own class (or function), with a common interface (e.g., they all have a `execute()` method or something). The context class then holds a reference to a strategy and uses it. To switch algorithms, you just swap out the strategy object.

Examples: - Sorting algorithms: You could have a Sorter context with a `sort()` method. It uses a strategy (bubble sort, quick sort, merge sort, etc.). You can pick which one based on data size or user preference. They all have the same interface (sort an array), but different implementations. - **Validation strategies**: For example, different password validation rules (strict vs lenient). - **Payment strategies** in an e-commerce system: PayPal, CreditCard, Bitcoin – each implements a `pay(amount)` method, and depending on user choice, the system uses the selected one. - **Compression strategies**: compress data using Zip, Rar, 7z – each with same interface but different algorithms. - **AI behaviors**: In a game, an enemy might have multiple strategies (aggressive, defensive, evading). You could swap the enemy's strategy to change its behavior without changing the rest of the code.

When and Why to Use Strategy

- **Multiple algorithms that can be used interchangeably**: If you find yourself needing different ways to do something and perhaps even choosing algorithm at runtime, strategy is apt.
- **Avoiding duplicate code**: If you have similar code branches that vary only by algorithm, separating them into strategies can reduce duplication.
- **Open/Closed Principle**: Adding a new strategy doesn't affect the context or other strategies. You can introduce new algorithms without modifying existing code (just create a new strategy class).
- **Simplify conditional logic**: Instead of one big method with lots of conditionals for different behaviors, you have separate classes.
- **Dynamic switching**: You can even change strategies on the fly if needed (e.g., change compression strategy if network conditions change).

The why: It provides **flexibility and clarity**. Each algorithm is in its own place (single responsibility), and the context is simpler. It also promotes composition over inheritance: the context uses a strategy rather than subclassing itself for different behaviors.

How to Implement Strategy in JS

We can use classes or just objects with certain methods, or even plain functions (since JS functions can be passed around).

Let's use a function example first (which is common in JS):

Imagine we have a text processing context that can format text in different ways: say uppercase, lowercase, or dash-separated (slug). We'll use functions for that.

```
// Strategies as simple functions
function formatUpper(text) {
  return text.toUpperCase();
}
```

```
function formatLower(text) {
  return text.toLowerCase();
}

function formatSlug(text) {
  return text.toLowerCase().replace(/\s+/g, '-');
}

// Context
class TextFormatter {
  constructor(formatStrategy) {
    this.strategy = formatStrategy;
  }

  setStrategy(formatStrategy) {
    this.strategy = formatStrategy;
  }

  format(text) {
    return this.strategy(text);
  }
}

// Usage:
const formatter = new TextFormatter(formatUpper);
console.log(formatter.format("Hello World")); // "HELLO
WORLD"

formatter.setStrategy(formatLower);
console.log(formatter.format("Hello World")); // "hello
world"

formatter.setStrategy(formatSlug);
console.log(formatter.format("Hello World")); //
"hello-world"
```

Here, `TextFormatter` is the context. It doesn't know how formatting is done; it just calls `this`). Initially, we give it `formatUpper` function. Later we switch to `formatLower` then `formatSlug`. We see the output change accordingly. We could add a new strategy, say `formatAlternateCaps`, by writing a new function and doing `formatter.setStrategy(formatAlternateCaps)` without touching the `TextFormatter` class.

Now an example with classes (if we wanted the strategies to have state or multiple methods):

Say we have a `PaymentProcessor` context that uses a strategy to process payment. Strategies could be classes like `PaypalStrategy`, `CreditCardStrategy`, each with a `pay(amount)` method.

```
// Strategy interface (not enforced in JS, but
conceptual):
class PaymentStrategy {
  pay(amount) {}
}

// Concrete strategies
class PaypalStrategy extends PaymentStrategy {
  constructor(email) {
    super();
    this.email = email;
  }

  pay(amount) {
    console.log(`Paying $${amount} via PayPal from
account ${this.email}`);
    // ... PayPal-specific code
  }
}
class CreditCardStrategy extends PaymentStrategy {
  constructor(cardNumber) {
    super();
    this.cardNumber = cardNumber;
  }
  pay(amount) {
    console.log(`Paying $${amount} via Credit Card
${this.cardNumber}`);
    // ... CC-specific code
  }
}

// Context
class Checkout {
  setPaymentStrategy(strategy) {
    this.paymentStrategy = strategy;
  }

  pay(amount) {
    if (!this.paymentStrategy) {
```

```
      throw new Error("Payment strategy not set");
    }

    this.paymentStrategy.pay(amount);
  }
}

// Usage:
const checkout = new Checkout();
checkout.setPaymentStrategy(new
PaypalStrategy("user@example.com"));
checkout.pay(100); // Paying $100 via PayPal from
account user@example.com

checkout.setPaymentStrategy(new
CreditCardStrategy("4111-1111-1111-1111"));
checkout.pay(75);  // Paying $75 via Credit Card 4111-
1111-1111-1111
```

The `Checkout` context doesn't know details of PayPal or credit cards. It just calls `strategy.pay(amount)`. We could add a new `CryptoStrategy` implementing `pay(amount)` for Bitcoin, and just do `checkout.setPaymentStrategy(new CryptoStrategy(walletAddress))` to use it. No changes to Checkout needed.

Visual Diagram

```
            +-----------------+
Context ->| Strategy        | (abstract interface)
            |    ^       ^    |
            |    |       |    |
            StrategyA  StrategyB ... (concrete strategies)
```

The **Context** has a reference to a **Strategy** (one of the concrete ones, but it treats it through the abstract interface). The context does something like `strategy.execute()` inside its own methods.

So:

```
context.method() {
    strategy.algorithm();
}
```

The effect is context's behavior changes depending on which strategy it's using.

Analogy

One analogy: **Transportation strategies** for travel. Suppose you have a navigator app (context) that can route you from A to B. The strategy can be driving, walking, cycling, public transit. Each has a different algorithm to find a route (drive on roads vs walk on static bus schedules). The app allows you to select the mode (strategy), then it gives you directions accordingly. The interface for the app to get directions is the same (start point, end point, get route), but internally it uses the strategy's algorithm to compute the route. You can swap strategies (change mode) and get a different result.

Another. **Payment method** example we did is a real-world analogy – different ways to pay, same interface of paying an amount.

Also, think about **sorting a list**: you can specify a custom comparison function in many languages. For example, `array.sort(compareFunction)` in JS. The array sorting algorithm is the context (it will run QuickSort or something under the hood, but uses your compare function to decide order). You provided a strategy (compare function) for ordering. Without providing one, it might default to lexicographic compare. If you provide a numeric compare or a custom one, it changes outcome. The sort method is a bit special since it's not swapping out the entire algorithm, just a part (the comparison), but it's the same idea of injecting a behavior.

Pitfalls

- **Over-engineering**: If you only ever need one algorithm, no need for strategy. Sometimes people introduce strategy prematurely. YAGNI (you ain't gonna need it) – don't add extra abstraction until there's a clear need for flexibility.
- **Context must know when to use which**: The pattern itself doesn't tell you how to choose a strategy; that logic could be outside (like user chooses) or inside context (like context

measures input size and picks a sort algorithm). That selection logic can sometimes be complex.

- **Performance**: A small overhead for the indirection of calling through a strategy object or function. Usually negligible. But if your strategies are tiny (like a small math formula), calling a function for it might be slower than just inlining a couple formulas with an if. It's a trade-off of clarity vs speed; rarely a big issue though.
- **Stateful strategies**: If strategies have state (like a strategy that counts how many times it's used or stores partial results), be careful if one instance is reused across contexts or calls. Usually strategies are stateless algorithms, or you give each context its own strategy instance.
- **Testing**: Strategies are easy to unit test in isolation (good!). But if the context sets up the wrong strategy or doesn't use it properly, that's something to test at integration. For example, if you forgot to call `strategy.method()` in context, it won't do anything and might go unnoticed.

Strategy is common in JS as higher-order functions or simply passing callbacks. For example, array's `.filter(predicate)` method lets you provide a strategy (the predicate function) to decide which items to keep. The array doesn't know your criteria; you supply a strategy.

Alright, next pattern: Command, which encapsulates requests as objects, enabling things like undo and queuing.

Command – Encapsulating Actions as Objects

The **Command pattern** turns a request or action into a stand-alone object that contains all information about the request. This allows you to parameterize methods with different requests, delay or queue the execution of requests, and support undoable operations. In simpler terms, think of each command object as a verb (an action to be taken) that you can pass around like data.

What Problem Does It Solve?

It decouples the object that needs something done (the invoker) from the object that knows how to do it (the receiver). Also, by making the request an object, you can log it, store it, or manipulate it.

Key scenarios: - **Undo/Redo**: Each command can have an `undo()` method that reverses its effect. If you have a stack of executed commands, you can call undo on the last ones to roll back. - **Action history or logging**: Since each action is an object, you can keep a list of them (for debugging or audit trail). - **Queuing and Scheduling**: You can queue command objects to be executed later or in a specific order. E.g., a batch job system might queue command objects representing tasks. - **Dynamic execution**: You can build lists of commands at runtime and execute them later, perhaps based on certain conditions or input (like scripting). - **Macro commands**: You can create a command that itself contains a sequence of other commands (composite pattern + command), to execute multiple things as one operation.

In GUIs, commands are often used for menu and button actions. The UI element triggers a command rather than having hardcoded logic, which makes it easier to enable/disable that UI element, reuse it, or map it to hotkeys, etc.

When and Why to Use Command

- **You need undo/redo**: Designing commands with an `undo` is a classic approach. For example, a text editor's every edit (typing, deleting, formatting) is a command that can be undone.
- **Decoupling UI from logic**: The UI elements (Invoker) shouldn't need to know business logic. They can just trigger a command. The command knows what to do (with which receiver).
- **Batching operations**: If you need to batch operations (like a series of database updates that can be done later or retried), commands can be enqueued.

- **Multi-level operations**: You might have a system where one operation triggers a series of sub-operations. Representing them as commands can make it easier to manage (e.g., if step 3 fails, you could undo steps 1-2).
- **Asynchronous execution**: Maybe you want to send tasks to a worker thread or server. If you represent tasks as command objects, you can easily serialize them or send them across.
- **Macro recording**: You want to let users record a sequence of actions and replay them (like Photoshop macro or Office macro). If every action is a Command, you can store the sequence and execute later.

Why: It **increases flexibility and extensibility**. You can add new commands easily (just new classes) without altering existing ones. It simplifies invokers – for example, a generic toolbar can trigger any command without knowing what it does; it just calls `execute`. And undo becomes feasible by tracking command objects.

How to Implement Command in JS

Define a Command class/interface with (usually) an `execute()` method. Optionally an `undo()` method (and sometimes a `redo()` which often just calls execute again or calls execute differently). The command will typically have references to the receiver(s) it needs and any data for the action.

The invoker (like a button or menu) will have a command assigned to it and just call `command.execute()` when clicked.

Example: Let's implement a simple light switch example, with a Light (receiver) and commands to turn it on and off. We'll support undo as well.

```
// Receiver
class Light {
  on() {
    console.log("The light is on");
  }

  off() {
```

```javascript
    console.log("The light is off");
  }
}

// Command interface
class Command {
  execute() {}
  undo() {}
}

// Concrete commands
class LightOnCommand extends Command {
  constructor(light) {
    super();
    this.light = light;
  }

  execute() {
    this.light.on();
  }

  undo() {
    this.light.off();
  }
}
class LightOffCommand extends Command {
  constructor(light) {
    super();
    this.light = light;
  }

  execute() {
    this.light.off();
  }

  undo() {
    this.light.on();
  }
}

// Invoker
class RemoteControl {
  setCommand(command) {
    this.command = command;
  }

  pressButton() {
```

```
    this.command.execute();
    this.lastCommand = this.command;
  }

  pressUndo() {
    if (this.lastCommand) {
      this.lastCommand.undo();
      this.lastCommand = null;
    }
  }
}

// Usage:
const lamp = new Light();
const remote = new RemoteControl();

remote.setCommand(new LightOnCommand(lamp));
remote.pressButton(); // The light is on
remote.pressUndo();   // The light is off

remote.setCommand(new LightOffCommand(lamp));
remote.pressButton(); // The light is off
remote.pressUndo();   // The light is on
```

In this example: - `Light` is the receiver of the request (it knows how to turn on/off). - `LightOnCommand` and `LightOffCommand` encapsulate the action of turning the light on or off. Each holds a reference to the `Light` and calls the appropriate method on it. They also implement `undo()` by doing the reverse action. - `RemoteControl` is the invoker. It doesn't know about Light's internals, it just knows if it has a command, it can execute it. We gave it a memory (`lastCommand`) to support a single-step undo. - We demonstrated how pressing the button executes the command, and pressing undo calls the command's undo.

In a UI, you might have multiple slots in the remote (like multiple buttons), each with its own command.

We could also implement a more JS-like approach: using functions as commands. For example, the command could be a function `() =>` `light.on()` for turn on, and store another for undo. But pairing them in an object (with execute/undo) clarifies the relationship.

Another example: Suppose we have a text editor with a text buffer. We can have commands like `InsertCommand`, `DeleteCommand` that carry out changes on the buffer and store the position and text affected to allow undo (delete would store what was deleted so it can insert it back, insert would store what was inserted so it can remove it).

Visual Diagram

```
[Invoker] -> [Command] -> [Receiver]
```

- The **Invoker** asks the **Command** to execute. It doesn't know what that means in detail.
- The **Command** knows which **Receiver** to operate on and what action to perform (it may also have stored parameters).
- After execution, the invoker can also ask the command to undo if needed.

We often also show a **Client** that creates the Command and sets it on the Invoker. For example, in our usage, we acted as client by doing `remote.setCommand(new LightOnCommand(lamp))`. In a UI framework, the wiring of commands to UI elements could be done at initialization (client code).

One neat aspect: Because commands are objects, you can have a list of them. For macro command, you could have a `MacroCommand` that has an array of commands and its execute calls execute on each, and its undo calls undo on each (in reverse order perhaps).

Analogy

One analogy: **Restaurant orders**. The waiter takes your order (writes on a ticket). That ticket is like a Command object: it has what dish to make and any special instructions. The chef (receiver) reads the ticket and executes it (cooks the dish). The waiter (invoker) doesn't cook, they just deliver the order to the chef. The ticket could be saved (for records, or if the customer says the dish is wrong, they check what was ordered). If the customer cancels the order early, the waiter can void that ticket (undo before it's made). Restaurants even allow sending a dish back (undo after execution) in some cases: the chef might then use the ticket info to know what to throw out or redo.

Another: **Commands in a video game console**. Pressing buttons on a controller sends commands to the game (like "jump", "shoot"). The game might queue those if needed or process immediately. If there's a rollback (like rewinding gameplay), the game might undo the commands.

Pitfalls

- **Lots of classes**: If your system has many distinct actions, you'll have many command classes. This can be boilerplate-heavy. In dynamic languages like JS, you can cut down on classes by using closures or a generic Command class that takes functions for execute/undo. But the pattern emphasizes clarity by separating them.
- **State in commands**: Commands may need to store state for undo (like what text was deleted). This can increase memory usage if a lot of commands are stored for undo. Also, if an undo depends on system state not stored (e.g., a command that queries something dynamically on execute but doesn't store it for undo), undo might not truly revert state.
- **Complex undo**: Some actions are not easily reversible. You have to design carefully. E.g., "send email" command – undo might not be possible if the email already sent. In such cases, you might not allow undo or have compensating actions (like send a follow-up "ignore last email" message).
- **Error handling**: If a command in a sequence fails (say in macro), how do you handle it? Possibly undo previous ones or stop further execution – logic needed.
- **Security**: If you expose command objects, ensure they can't be misused. For example, if commands can be serialized to JSON for networking, someone could alter that to call methods they shouldn't. Usually you don't expose raw commands externally without validation.

In JavaScript apps, explicit Command pattern might be seen in: - Redux actions (they are data describing what happened – similar to commands without methods, reducers act on them). - Automation scripts: e.g., browser automation (each step is a command: click, type, etc. and can be recorded). - Undoable operations: some frameworks or libraries might implement operations as commands to facilitate undo (like Draft.js for rich text had a command concept for editor actions). - Game engines in JS, or any editor (graphics, text) often use commands.

Alright, now for the State pattern, which is about an object changing its behavior by changing its internal state object.

State – An Object with Many Faces

The **State pattern** allows an object to alter its behavior when its internal state changes, as if the object's class changed at runtime. In other words, instead of using a lot of `if/else` or `switch` to check what state something is in and then behaving accordingly, you delegate those behaviors to state objects. The context has a current state, and it delegates to it. When the state changes, you swap the state object.

What Problem Does It Solve?

When an object's behavior is significantly influenced by its state, and it has multiple states, you often get big conditional statements in methods:

```
if (state === "draft") { ... }
else if (state === "published") { ... }
else if (state === "archived") { ... }
```

This logic might be spread across many methods (each doing something different based on state). It becomes messy and hard to maintain, especially if new states are added.

State pattern organizes this by giving each state its own class (or object) with the behavior for that state. The context holds a reference to a state object and delegates methods to it. Each state class implements the same interface of operations, but in a way specific to that state.

Also, the transitions between states can be controlled or encapsulated: the state object might decide when to transition to another state.

Examples: - **TCP Connection**: states like Closed, Connecting, Open, Closing. Methods `open()`, `send()`, `close()` do different things in each state (open while closed opens connection; open while connecting might wait; open while open does nothing or error; etc.). - **Document workflow**: Draft, Moderation, Published. The `edit()` method might be allowed in Draft, not in Published; `publish()` does something in Draft state (like transitions to Published), but if you call `publish()` when already Published, maybe it does nothing or logs a warning. - **UI Mode**: e.g., an application with modes (selection mode, drawing mode). The click event handling could be different in each mode. Instead of `if (mode===draw) draw(); else if (mode===select) select();`, you can have a state object for current mode that has a `onClick()` method do the right thing. - **ATMs**: States: CardNotInserted, CardInserted, PINEntered, DispensingCash, etc. Behavior for `insertCard`, `enterPin`, `requestCash` differ based on current state. - **Simple**: Turnstile gate: Locked state and Unlocked state. If locked and you insert a coin, it unlocks (transition to Unlocked state); if locked and you push, alarm or nothing happens; if unlocked and you push, it opens (and transitions to Locked); if unlocked and you insert another coin, maybe it returns coin or just thanks.

When and Why to Use State

- **Complex conditional state-dependent code**: If you have an object that behaves differently in different modes or states, and the differences are enough to justify separate logic.
- **Want to simplify code**: State pattern moves each bit of behavior into its own class, making code easier to manage and extend.

- **Adding states easily**: If you foresee adding new states, state pattern is useful because you can create a new class for the new state without breaking existing ones. If using conditionals, adding a state means hunting down all `if` statements and adding branches.
- **Avoiding duplication**: Often different states have slight variations, but some shared logic. With state classes, you can sometimes use inheritance or composition to share code between states (e.g., common functionality in an abstract state base class).
- **Controlled transitions**: If the transitions between states are complex (not every state can go to every other state directly), the state objects can enforce that by deciding the next state or refusing an invalid transition.

Why: It **improves maintainability and clarity**. Instead of one class with tons of conditional logic, you have many classes each focused on one state's logic. It aligns with single responsibility (each state class handles behavior for one state). It also can make state transitions explicit and controlled.

How to Implement State in JS

We need: - A **State interface** that defines what methods the context will call that depend on state. - Concrete **State classes** for each state, implementing those methods. - A **Context** class that has a current state (initially some default) and possibly a way to change state (often via a method or maybe the state objects set the context's state when transitions happen).

Let's design a simple example: a **Vending Machine** with states: `NoCoinState`, `HasCoinState`, `SoldState` (dispensing an item), and maybe a `SoldOutState` if we want to handle empty machine.

We will implement methods: `insertCoin()`, `pressButton()`, `dispense()`. The behavior of these methods depends on the state: - In NoCoinState: `insertCoin` will accept coin and transition to HasCoin. `pressButton` will do nothing (you need to insert coin).

dispense does nothing. - In HasCoinState: insertCoin maybe rejects additional coin or says "already have coin". pressButton will transition to SoldState (to dispense). dispense in HasCoin maybe says "press button first". - In SoldState: (item is being dispensed) The machine will actually release the item and then go to either NoCoin (if items left) or SoldOut (if that was last item). During SoldState, maybe insertCoin and pressButton are temporarily ignored or queued. - SoldOutState: All items sold, insertCoin returns coin, pressButton does nothing, etc.

For brevity, I'll do NoCoin, HasCoin, and Sold (dispensing) and skip a detailed SoldOut.

```
class VendingMachine; // forward reference

// State interface (using ES6 class syntax for clarity)
class VendingState {
  insertCoin(machine) {}
  pressButton(machine) {}
  dispense(machine) {}
}

// Concrete States
class NoCoinState extends VendingState {
  insertCoin(machine) {
    console.log("Coin inserted.");
    machine.setState(new HasCoinState());
  }

  pressButton(machine) {
    console.log("You pressed the button, but no coin
inserted.");
  }

  dispense(machine) {
    console.log("Insert coin first.");
  }
}

class HasCoinState extends VendingState {
  insertCoin(machine) {
    console.log("Coin already inserted. Can't insert
another.");
  }
```

```
  pressButton(machine) {
    console.log("Button pressed... dispensing now.");
    machine.setState(new SoldState());
    machine.dispense(); // proceed to dispense after
changing state
  }

  dispense(machine) {
    console.log("No item dispensed. Press the
button.");
  }
}

class SoldState extends VendingState {
  insertCoin(machine) {
    console.log("Please wait, dispensing in
progress.");
  }

  pressButton(machine) {
    console.log("Already dispensing an item.");
  }

  dispense(machine) {
    if (machine.itemCount > 0) {
      console.log("An item comes rolling out!");
      machine.itemCount--;
    }

    if (machine.itemCount > 0) {
      machine.setState(new NoCoinState());
    } else {
      console.log("Machine is now out of items.");
      machine.setState(new NoCoinState()); // would be
SoldOutState in a full design
    }
  }
}

// Context
class VendingMachine {
  constructor(itemCount) {
    this.itemCount = itemCount;
    this.state = new NoCoinState();
  }
```

65

```
  setState(state) {
    this.state = state;
  }

  insertCoin() {
    this.state.insertCoin(this);
  }

  pressButton() {
    this.state.pressButton(this);
  }

  dispense() {
    this.state.dispense(this);
  }
}

// Usage:
const machine = new VendingMachine(2);
machine.pressButton();     // You pressed the button,
but no coin inserted.
machine.insertCoin();      // Coin inserted.
machine.insertCoin();      // Coin already inserted.
Can't insert another.
machine.pressButton();     // Button pressed...
dispensing now. \n An item comes rolling out!
machine.pressButton();     // You pressed the button,
but no coin inserted. (since now NoCoinState again)
machine.insertCoin();      // Coin inserted.
machine.pressButton();     // Button pressed...
dispensing now. \n An item comes rolling out! \n
Machine is now out of items.
machine.insertCoin();      // Coin inserted. (In our
design, we reuse NoCoinState even if empty)
```

Output would be like:

```
You pressed the button, but no coin inserted.
Coin inserted.
Coin already inserted. Can't insert another.
Button pressed... dispensing now.
An item comes rolling out!
You pressed the button, but no coin inserted.
Coin inserted.
Button pressed... dispensing now.
An item comes rolling out!
Machine is now out of items.
```

```
Coin inserted.
```

Notice how the behavior changed depending on `state`. We didn't have to write `if (state===HasCoin)` inside `pressButton` method; instead, `pressButton()` is a method on the state classes.

We kind of cheated by using `machine.dispense()` inside `HasCoinState.pressButton` after switching state to SoldState. This is a common pattern: the press of the button triggers dispense sequence, so we switched to SoldState and then immediately called dispense. Alternatively, we could have had the Machine call dispense itself after pressButton returns some indicator.

If we had a `SoldOutState`, we'd switch to that when items go to 0, and in SoldOutState, `insertCoin` would probably reject coin.

One might note we could optimize state objects by reusing instances (since in this design they don't hold unique data, just behavior). But often it's fine to instantiate new ones on transitions (especially if transitions are rare relative to actions). Or state instances could be singletons (one instance of each) if no unique info is needed per context.

Visual Diagram

Imagine the states and transitions like a state machine diagram:

```
          insertCoin                   pressButton
[NoCoin] ------------> [HasCoin] -----------> [Sold]
   ^                    pressButton|          (dispense
done)
   |                           (dispense)         |
   |-------------------------------------------------- (to
NoCoin)
```

Each **State** class implements the same interface (insertCoin, pressButton, dispense). The **Context** (VendingMachine) has a reference to a current state object. When context.insertCoin() is called, it delegates to `this.state.insertCoin(this)`.

The state method might change the context's state via `machine.setState(new SomeState)` to transition. Or the context might change the state based on a return value. Here we let state handle it.

Analogy

The water analogy: **water changing states** (solid, liquid, gas) is often used. Water behaves differently in different states: as a solid (ice) it has a fixed shape, as a liquid it flows, as a gas it expands. Imagine a `Water` object with a state. If it's in SolidState, a method like `heat()` might transition it to LiquidState at 0°C, and if in LiquidState then `heat()` transitions to GasState at 100°C. The actions possible could be `moldShape()` (only valid in solid), `pour()` (valid in liquid), etc., which would either be no-ops or errors in the wrong state. Using State pattern, each state class (IceState, WaterState, VaporState) handles those actions appropriately (maybe IceState allows moldShape but not pour, etc.).

Another analogy: **Phone** modes. Old cell phones had profiles: silent, vibrate, loud. In SilentState, when a call comes in (`receiveCall` method), it might just log it (no sound, no vibration). In VibrateState, `receiveCall` triggers vibration. In LoudState, `receiveCall` plays a ringtone. The phone can change state (user sets the profile). Without state pattern, you'd have `if(profile===silent)` inside `receiveCall`. With state pattern, you have separate classes for each profile.

Also, **traffic light** example from earlier: Red, Green, Yellow states, each with a `tick()` method that decides when to transition to next color.

Pitfalls

- **Overkill for simple cases**: If an object only has two states and trivial differences, using state pattern might be unnecessary overhead (two classes, etc.). A simple boolean and an if might do. But as soon as logic grows or more states appear, state pattern helps.

- **More objects**: You end up with several state classes which could be many if states are numerous. However, often states are limited (if it's truly like modes of an entity).
- **State transitions visibility**: It might be a bit less obvious reading the context code how states transition, since the logic can be inside state classes. You have to read those classes to follow possible transitions. Good documentation or state diagrams help.
- **Sharing data**: The context likely has data (like our `itemCount` in machine) that state objects might use. Here we passed `machine` into state methods to allow state to modify context. Some purists might instead let context orchestrate transitions (like state returns an indicator, and context switches state). But giving state a pointer to context (as we did) is common. It introduces some circularity: context has state, state calls context. It's okay if done carefully.
- **Reusability of states**: If state objects are stateless (no instance vars except context), you could reuse one instance across all contexts of that type. But if states need to hold something (maybe a timestamp when entered or a count of something), then each context needs its own instance. We often just create new ones on transitions as needed.
- **Testing**: You can unit test state classes individually by giving them a mock or fake context to operate on. That's good. But testing the whole context might require simulating sequences to ensure it transitions properly. A state machine can have many paths, so ensure coverage of transitions.
- **Alternate implementations**: Sometimes the State pattern can be achieved using function tables or objects of functions without full classes. For instance, an object with state can have a property that references an object with methods (the state behaviors). Changing state could mean assigning a different object to that property. That's essentially the same idea but using a plain object as state representation. It can be lighter weight but less explicit.

State pattern is essentially an elegant way to implement state machines or mode# Essential Software Design Patterns for JavaScript Developers

Conclusion

We've now toured through a collection of essential design patterns and seen how they can be applied in JavaScript. Each pattern addresses a specific recurring problem in software design, providing a template for how to structure a solution. By using these patterns, we gain several benefits in our architecture: - **Improved Communication:** Design patterns give us a shared vocabulary. We can say "let's use an Observer here" or "this class is a Facade," and other developers familiar with patterns immediately grasp the concept. This makes discussions and code reviews more efficient, because we don't have to explain everything from scratch; the name of the pattern tells a story. - **Modularity and Decoupling:** Many patterns (Factory, Strategy, Observer, Mediator, etc.) are about reducing tight coupling. This leads to code that's easier to change and extend. For example, because we used Strategy, we can add a new algorithm without rewriting the context; because we used Observer, we can add a new subscriber without touching the publisher. Patterns often enforce one of the SOLID principles, like open/closed or single responsibility, which improves modularity. - **Flexibility and Extensibility:** Patterns like Decorator, Command, and State show how to design for growth. We can add new decorators (features), new commands (operations), or new states without modifying existing code, following the open/closed principle. This means our codebase can evolve with fewer breaking changes. - **Encapsulation of Complexity:** Patterns such as Facade and Adapter demonstrate how to hide complexity behind a simple interface. This not only makes usage easier for other parts of the code but also localizes complex code, making it easier to debug or optimize without affecting other parts of the system. For instance, if the subsystem behind a Facade changes, we adjust the Facade but the rest of the code remains untouched. - **Reusability:** By decoupling components, patterns often make it possible to reuse components in different contexts. A class that communicates via a Mediator doesn't depend on concrete classes, so you could reuse it in a different app with a different mediator. A well-implemented Strategy is usable in many contexts requiring that algorithm. And a single Observer subject can have many different observers over its lifetime. - **Ease of Testing:** Decoupled code is often easier to unit test. For example, with Strategy, you can test each strategy independently. With Observer, you can simulate events and verify observers react. With Command, you can test execute/undo logic in isolation. Patterns encourage separating concerns, which usually translates to simpler tests for each piece. - **Architectural Vision:** Using patterns forces you to think at a higher level about how parts of your system interact. Instead of ad-hoc solutions, you approach problems with tried-and-true templates, which often results in a cleaner architecture. It's like having a set of architectural plans for common building types – you can of course build without them, but having them speeds up the process and results in fewer structural issues.

On the flip side, it's important to remember: **patterns are tools, not goals**. Don't force a pattern where a simple solution would suffice. Over-architecting with patterns can lead to unnecessary complexity (sometimes jokingly called "patternitis"). Always consider if a pattern truly makes the code better (cleaner, more flexible, easier to understand) or if it's being used just for the sake of it.

For example, if you have just two classes that need to interact, you probably don't need a Mediator. Or if you have one configuration object in your app, making it a formal Singleton might be overkill (module exports might be enough). Use the simplest solution that works, but keep patterns in mind for when complexity grows or certain problems appear.

Design patterns also evolve with programming paradigms. We focused on classic GoF patterns in an object-oriented context, but in JavaScript (which blends OO and functional), you might implement some patterns differently (like using higher-order functions for Strategy or using module patterns for Singleton). The essence remains, even if the implementation is more function-based or uses modern language features.

Additionally, many frameworks implement these patterns under the hood so you don't have to reinvent them. For instance, in React, the Context API combined with hooks can serve as a Mediator/Observer for state across components. In Redux, the store and actions are essentially the Mediator and Command patterns. Recognizing that helps you understand those frameworks more deeply.

In your day-to-day coding, you likely apply patterns unconsciously. Event handlers? That's Observer. Swap a function implementation? Strategy. Want a single instance? Module/Singleton. Use a library to wrap different API calls? Facade/Adapter. Understanding the formal pattern behind these will help you communicate and reason about your code more effectively.

Finally, design patterns encourage thinking about **software architecture** rather than just individual lines of code. They are about the big picture and the interactions. By mastering these patterns, you start to see higher-level solutions to problems and write code that stands the test of time. Architecture isn't just about choosing frameworks or microservices; it's also present in how you design the classes and modules in a single application.

To sum up, design patterns are like well-traveled roads in software design. Following them can help you avoid dead ends and potholes that others have already encountered. They provide a balance between quick-and-dirty and over-engineered solutions. With a pattern, you get a solution that is known to work, is flexible for future change, and is generally understood by experienced developers.

As you continue in your journey as a JavaScript developer, you'll find these patterns (and others beyond the basics covered here) incredibly useful. But always apply them judiciously – the goal is to write **readable, maintainable, and efficient** code. Patterns are one of the tools in your toolbox to achieve that.

Essential Software Design Patterns for JavaScript Developers

JS

Victor Bona